# LIFE LYRICS

## Love, Sex & Other Deviances

### *Melody Fowler*

authorHOUSE®

*AuthorHouse*™
*1663 Liberty Drive*
*Bloomington, IN 47403*
*www.authorhouse.com*
*Phone: 1-800-839-8640*

*First published by AuthorHouse     05/23/2011*

*ISBN: 978-1-4520-7665-2  (sc)*
*ISBN: 978-1-4520-7666-9( hc)*
*ISBN: 978-1-4520-7667-6 (e)*

*Library of Congress Control Number: 2011907578*

*Printed in the United States of America*

*Any people depicted in stock imagery provided by Thinkstock are models, and such images are being used for illustrative purposes only. Certain stock imagery © Thinkstock.*

This is dedicated to
all the people who believed in me
before I knew how to believe in myself;

My Mother, Anna Tanner,
You will always be my greatest inspiration.

# Contents

# LOTUS FLOWERS

Worldwide we are prisoners of our sex

     We FEMALES

The pain is great and is small for us all


Widows of India living a half life

Some too young to have lain with their

     husbands as a true wife

Lovely Lotus Flowers they float gracefully

     imprisoned in the shadows

They drift in the dark & dank waters

     of their existence

Still beautiful and resilient

Tragically they pray to the gods

     that they might be reborn a man

How can it be, that man cannot embrace

     the sex that births the human race?

*Do you fear our power?*

Young African girls
Tiny blossoms sliced with rusty razors
Uninformed

Saturated with blood, tears and fear

Their tortured cries no one will choose to

hear Fate forever denies pleasure

Instead there is a life of pain

Who could possibly see this as just?

       Why is it wrong for women to lust?

*Do you fear our power?*

Chinese baby girls left in the elements

       to die

Men cannot reproduce alone

They need us like flesh and like bone

*Do you fear our power?*

Burquas block the light

Buds need sun to grow

Just as a son needs a Mother

We all need a reason to be

2

And all have a right to be free

*Do you fear our power?*
Women in the Western world still earn less

Do they really see us as less?

Or do they desire that WE see us as less?

They look at us and think of what position

     they could contort us in

Then we are made to feel that

     we are the ones that are made of sin
Worldwide you whore us however you can
I ask you to remember this:

It is MOTHER earth

And WE that give birth

If you kill us, you too will be gone

*You should not fear our power – Embrace it*
We do not desire war

We do not wish to dominate you

We can

And will

Love you

If you see

The greatest power

Is

EQUALITY

# 2 SIDES OF I

I am the product of two sides

of one culture

One, born of privilege and

a sense of entitlement

The other, humble and hardworking

I am my Mother's desire

for fine things

and

My Father's sweat into the soil

Her French manicure and

the dirt under His nails

How do I reconcile my identity in this contrast of culture?

I am equal parts pride and shame

His ethics I value and

hers I oppose

I bow my head

This symbolic gesture communicates

two things:

Own personal shame and respect,

my ethnicity's disparity

I honor my Father, he is reverence and love

I avoid my Mother,

she is judgment and pain

He requests that I heal my relationship

with his wife

I cannot deny him anything

That is in my capacity to give him in this life

He is my core and my substance

She is unfathomable

We don't look or think alike

I believe behind her light skin

is my dark side

Most curse inherited physicality

For me it's the inner recesses I wish to reject

The negative dialogue echoes in my head

Forgiving her will soothe him

and release me

I recognize to be whole I must resolve

I am 2 sides of 1

Let the absolution begin

Without her

I never would have known

the great love of him

I forgive you Mother

2 became 1

that makes me whole

Amen

# BLUE

I saw blue this evening

And that blue was all there was

Solid and beautiful

Fighting black

As it moves in a mist

Night black robbing the beauty of the evening blue

It was an endless patch of hope

If I were a color I would want to be that Lavender blue

# FAITH AND RELIGION

Faith and Religion

One has little to do with the other

I know all about

quiet controlled environments

Where there is quiet

there isn't always peace

The confessionals

The small dark closets

Musty with fear, shame, regret

AND

sheer desperation

Men in black clothes

AND

white collars

They squashed the good girl in me

with their judgment

For a time there was comfort

in the rich tone of the bells

summoning the flock

The soothing scent of frankincense

the hymns of faith and forgiveness

It was a place of solace

I did hide there

Then after all the years of ritual,

Catholic school

Relatives on their moral high ground

Making themselves feel big

AND

trying their best

to make me feel

*small*

All that remains is

the Guilt

It was hammered into my soul

like the nails through His flesh on the cross

What was the cost?

I kept faith

And

let go of religion

I believe in being kind to others and

leaving things better than

I found them

Love is my religion

If only I could let go of

the Guilt

# KNOW-IT-ALL

Arrogant and uncaring and PROUD of it

There is a difference between knowledge

    and WISDOM

You please yourself hurling backhanded

    comments wearing that

        superior smirk

Insults are what they really are

    but not to my intelligence

        to yours

The evil grin says you have no feeling

    of equality

You come from a culture of "me"

You toot your own horn like you are

      performing part of a symphony

As though it would delight those listening

And if there is anything WE don't care about, it is to listen to your soliloquy of:

"I did..."   "I know..."   "I told him..."

"I...  I...   I"

You should recognize you love the sound

      of your own voice

         and spare the rest of us

Part of earning respect

      is knowing to get it you must know how to GIVE it

But you don't care what we feel

That's good

      because you don't have our respect

The years shall pass

If life teaches you the bare necessities:

You will know that caring is vital to personal growth

      ...and one day

         If fate sees fit

You will see this younger self in another -

You will distinguish how little you really

      knew

When you knew it all

## STUPID HUMANS

If I had a dollar for every

stupid human I encountered...

I would own my own island

I would live in a castle on

said island

Instead...

I have high blood pressure.

# SPIRIT THIEF

You'll never be anything

**He said**

The words were poison

They infected my life

Index finger in **MY** face

Making sure I knew **MY** place

raised voice

*Apparently* **I** didn't listen to quiet reason


Pressing buttons

Especially the ones marked

"Danger! Don't press."

The ones marked with skull and crossbones

They are pressed over and over and over

The buttons eventually are broken permanently in the "on" position

**AND STILL**

He couldn't break me
You're a WHORE

**He said**

Who died and made him the boss of me?

Oh yes.  My Dad died.

My Mom became **his** bride

And he became the boss of *us*.
All his pontificating on the evils of **ME**

Beat me emotionally

And she

robotic and empty

A shell of who she used to be

Systematically erasing her and trying to destroy me

The light that shone so bright in **us**

He tried to extinguish

Squeezing it like it was pus

Doubt and insecurity reigned

Medicating myself to ease the pain

My SPIRIT refused to die

It like a pilot light

The flicker lay in wait

Spirit thieves only have the power we bestow unto
them

I began to release myself from his hold

I was eighteen, young and bold

There had to be more than this

I had to find my bliss
I met with her secretly

I have to leave

**I said**

To stay is death

I'll come with you

**She said**

**My** Spirit's flame ignited

Like the fiery red ball of the sun as it sets

A brilliant beacon of light

It revealed the path for our escape

She and me now free

You'll never be anything

**He said**

I will be **everything**

**I said**

**I**

**Am EVERYTHING**

And

He

Is

dead

# WHEN DREAMS MEET DAYLIGHT

In that place caught between

Wakefulness and sleep,

I catch a glimpse of images,

Like a mosaic of life;

Little glimpses of what was or possibly what might be,

When my eyes squint to arrive into this day I travel into
full consciousness,

I realize that some images were strong enough to cross
to the daylight with me...

Perhaps not dreams,

When they survive to consciousness,

They are like positive affirmations,
to guide our steps towards them.

# BALLERINA

She floats across the stage
      with the grace of a swan
Clear stiletto heels & brass pole
Easily replaced
 With Ballet slippers and a barre,
More to her taste
They see her in leather lingerie
She sees herself clad in
      silk and velvet finery
She is on another stage in her mind

She pauses to face the horny glares
But she's not there to return their stare

Mr Gyno-row

Depraved lost soul

He never misses a show

Eager to catch her eye

Her affections he tries to buy


But they are all faceless and nameless


Speakers blare guitar, heavy rock

The delicate aria of violins in her head;

 It doesn't block

Her body sways and bends

forming strong straight Dancer lines

Unappreciated by the patrons

    who she avoids like land mines

She pauses

to face their horny glares

but she's not there

to return their stare

She's writing up her grocery list

Bread – eggs – milk

Another spin on the pole

All the while wondering

if she took out the trash

This is what she does for cash

An hour a day,

a small price to pay

They in their fantasy and she in hers


She closes the door behind her

as she floats off the stage

She returns to her real life

The transition as simple as turning a page


The swan floats out the door and down

the street seeking her lake

In her sweatshirt and her jeans,

       dreaming her ballerina dreams

# BACKYARD BLISS

It's warm

The breeze carries the fragrance of the lilies and the sound of chimes in my gazebo; I laze in the reclining deck chair

Dividing my time between watching the inside of my eyelids and the sky divers in the distance

I read poetry, mostly Bukowski

I listen to the birds, and the barking dogs, the passing trains... peace washes over me

My thought is that we are all a little broken and that's what makes us beautiful

Bukowski and me, in my backyard bliss

Broken and beautiful

# THE VOICE

*Then*

My lips stretched to scream

    but it was not audible

This silent scream rang so loud in my head

    at times it stifled life

I wondered if I was invisible in this

    deafening quiet

A lifetime peering through the looking glass...

...but I did not fall down the rabbit hole

I journeyed there unwittingly and FACED

    the madness

To understand it was NOT mine

    It was theirs

They could not chain my mind

    because my spirit is FREE

_Now_

My voice is heard

They could not take it... it belongs to ME

The Scream is gone

Replaced

Now I sing


I sing my redemption song

I sing it proud, I sing it strong

I sing for others trapped in the silence

But not for long

THIS VOICE HAS PURPOSE

      AND WILL BE HEARD

They cannot clip the wings of this bird!

# IT'S NOT WHAT YOU THINK

**Seduced by it**

The lights, the riches,

surrounded by silicon bitches

**Eaten by it**

My trust, my faith, my soul

**Left empty by it**

Deconstructed, reconstructed;

Like I am made of paper

Ripped apart, piece by piece

     by crows

Then glued together;

The jagged ripped edges

 invisible to the world

What your eyes can't see

 my heart feels

When the dream becomes

a nightmare

I don't answer to my name

Does anyone remember Robyn?

She feels like a distant memory

They told me

They warned me

I have to remind myself I wanted it

**FAME**

It's not what you think

# MUSHROOM CLOUDS

Marching together we rally for peace

A mass, we are, growing like fungus

Shouting at the sky,

lifting our voices to the clouds

I stop and all sound disappears

Stepping back I watch the voiceless mob:

singing, chanting

Their words melt into the air

I look above my thoughts drifting

Making shapes with the clouds in my mind

Laughing children, smiling eyes

Souls that leave

without saying their goodbyes

Eagles, planes, missiles, bears,

blackened skies, barren land

Mushroom clouds

A child crying in the distance brings me back

The noise echoes

creating a wave of disturbance

in the atmosphere

Forming a blanket of white

smothering the mushroom cloud

Waving a flag for surrender

# NICE LIPS

"Nice Lips," your words hum,

As you kiss them

Moments in the now

And

In the long ago

 All one

You moan as you devour me

Until I convulse and

The pleasure sets me free

We stare into each other's souls

when you thrust into me

I feel you

      The way you want me to

You leave your imprint on me

Do you daydream about this

    Like I do?

Just thinking of all your intensity makes the blood rush

    and the wetness flow

Oh baby do you really know?

What exists between us

Is

Just

Pure

Energy

"Nice lips" your words hum,

As you kiss them.

# R U the I

R u the 1 I've looked 4?

R u the 1 I've longed 4?

Do you seek 2 give & not 2 take?

I know you relate

I've always been a gambler

The stakes are high – Do I dare roll the die

What came before you is eclipsed

It and he was nothing but a fantasy

but U r reality

Always darkest before the dawn

R my eyes closed?  Maybe u R the light?

How can this B?

R u the 1?

Or will I run? R u the 1?

Or do I lose everything

Is it my everything u want?

U will not claim me

2 the world

the whole thing looks shady

2 me it means I'm not ur baby

R u the 1?

I am like a child

spinning around with my eyes closed

When I open them I will fall down

Maybe it is time 4 me 2 leave this town

Maybe it won't hurt when u aren't around

I wanted u 2 b the 1

# WHAT I WANTED TO BELIEVE

I wanted 2 believe

Believe that I could enjoy just a piece of u

My piece of u

The piece that God saved 4 me

The piece fate delivered 2 me


But my heart isn't made that way


I am not the 1 of many type

I am not a girlfriend

I am THE girlfriend

You can't just play with me and put me

back on the shelf

I feel u baby.

I feel u in the heart of me

Not just the part of me u think about


Maybe 1 day

1 day when U r old and gray

Maybe that day

Maybe then U will want 2 slow down

Maybe I could be the 1


Right now I think

I am meant 2 b ur friend

so this is the end

# THE SUM

There is a disconnect

between US and THEM

US and THEM

I ponder this

These 2 words an anagram of

THE SUM

We are THE SUM of the two sides.

For US

The equation begins just like the Day

An assault of alarm sounding,

Feet hitting floor before eyes open,

water hitting skin forcing consciousness

*Letting caffeine & sugar fill the parts still*

*foggy*

*For THEM*

*Breakfast made, lunches packed, dinner*

*in slow-cooker, Permission slips signed*

*Arguments ensue for clothing choices*

*Finally ignition fired up*

*Off to daycare and school*

*FOR US*

*Journey to work wrought with ugly traffic*

*Witness THEM*

*Make lane changes without signaling*

*I shake fist representing*

*US*

*that do signal*

Log on to phone lines, hear THEM tell US

What should be done

How it should be handled if up to THEM

And they feel it unfortunate will be left up

to US

Read Email from THEM

Extolling merits of compliance

Which often will be met with Defiance  from

US

What then is THE SUM?

We have no control over THEM

Or forces that surround US

Another Anagram appears

THEM - US

THUS ME

*THE SUM THUS becomes up to ME*

*I will do what I can to take care of ME*

*THUS*

*I will be able to take care of THEM*

*The common denominator and*

*most important factor at the end of the day*

*ME*

*This much I know*

*Take a deep cleansing breath and*

*THE SUM*

*Will equal*

*THUS*

*That I don't lose*

*ME!*

# LUSH

You are LUSH

Like the scent of jasmine on a humid day

You carry me away

to places exotic

Like wine aged to perfection

You are meant to be savored

Like a ripe juicy strawberry

rich in flavor and color

You excite all my senses

You are all these things

Inviting and Intoxicating

I want LUSH

And You are LUSCIOUS

# REVELATION

You smell like exotic blossoms

Buried in your intoxicating fragrance

      are thorns

Brushing against you

      I risked piercing my skin

It allowed your poison

      to enter my bloodstream

Then your essence grew

      like terminal cancer

The pain spread and acted like fertilizer

It turned love into hate

It took my nurturing, sweet nature

      And justified my murderous thoughts

Your beauty is superficial

The only depth you have

    is infinite capacity for deception

Your taste is **sour**

Do you writhe wounded

    reading these words?

Or do rise like a demon Phoenix in anger?

Let me name this bitterness for you:

Karma

How does that taste in your mouth?

Is it anything like your cheap vodka?

You were quite credible for a time

But the light always reveals

    what the dark would have us believe

You said you've had everything but love

You are disingenuous

Understanding that you reap what you sow

The harvest of your true intentions will bring you the emptiness that is so deserved.

## I WANT ONLY THIS

I stand in the steam of the shower,

closing my eyes and willing you to be here.

The little droplets of water

   trickle lovingly down, and around all the little
   crevices of my body;

I imagine you in every drop;

Touching all my secret places.

My body whispers to you all the things

   I will not say out loud.

Do you want "more?"

No, lover, I want only this...

This can only live outside

   the confines of tradition

Don't ask me for the things

      the others want.

I want this lust preserved in its perfect, undisturbed state.

It would die exposed to the elements:

      the everyday, the bills...

      Oh, how that kills the thrills!

The rest of the world cannot understand

      and we don't expect them to.

The people that understand this are

the only ones that matter – me and you.

When you next stand in the steam

      of the shower

When you feel the little droplets.

Know I am there in every one of them.

# DYING EMBERS OF LOVE

It hurt to be apart

Now it hurts to be together

Your tongue is razor sharp

    and I am bleeding

I have so many memories

    Time shared with you

        Us Two

Once so stimulating

    Now excruciating

I try harder

Love more

You concede

Love less

One Reminisces romance

One evokes

    every hurtful word

        and moment

            as if it were sport

If this is a sport

    Then you my lover

        are a champion

I just want the bleeding to stop

# RIBBONS

Ribbons

Shredded to ribbons

Once a pretty bow with silver piping, glitter

and shimmer

Gone

Just tattered frayed threads

Attached to the memory

Holding on to the little bits

A reminder of what used to be

loved so

More than one could ever consciously know

Reality hit like a falling star

Why did it have to go this far?

# 100 POUNDS

My eyes are heavy

I'm so tired

Tired of carrying around all my stuff

Some people keep it deep

They chase it down with their favorite toxin

I've just carried mine around.

A monkey on a back doesn't sound

      so bad when you've carried around

      100 pounds

In my dreams I'm free –

      so light sometimes I even have wings

So when my eye lids are heavy

      I'm so glad to sleep

      When I slip away from this consciousness I'm free

I won't be carrying anything

I'll be soaring in the sky

I'll look down and see that 100 pounds

I'll see it sitting at the curb side

     waiting to be hauled away with the

     rest of the trash

I'll wonder why I carried it for so long

Maybe I thought if I carried it

     I wouldn't lose you

My memories are all I have left

Maybe if I let all the stuff go it would be like

pretending it didn't happen

Pretending you didn't happen

It and You happened

All that was lost was me

Somewhere in there

     was me

Deep inside that 100 pounds

# MY HEART WHISPERED

You were a year older
You were a world bolder
I watched hopeful
My heart whispered
**Notice me**

I was your friend
Secret was I wanted more
Wanted you to show me
Show me how to be more
When we slow danced I wasn't teasing
I was trying to show you
Show you I wanted more
My heart whispered
**Want me**

Once we shared a few tender awkward moments
But our teen lust was interrupted
Went on as friends
I kept my secret
School ended and our paths parted
My heart whispered
**Remember me**

In the darkness of a club

We were years older

You were still a world bolder

**You noticed me**


You asked if I remembered

I laughed, red-faced, and we danced

Though we parted

My heart sang

**You remembered me**


Decades older

Now I am a world bolder

You found me on a web site

**Did I remember you?**


My heart sang

Show me

A woman now but still 14 inside

Still want you to show me...

Show me how to be more

**I'm not whispering anymore**

# THE HEARTBREAKER AND THE HEARTBROKEN

The Heartbreaker and the Heartbroken

Interchangeable

We've taken turns at being both

We give as good as we get

We find it all so hard to forget

We're a puzzle

Although jagged the Pieces match together

And yet we still get cut

And yet we still bleed

But we manage to heal

Scars map out our mutual understanding

And we mend what is broken in us


We appreciate each other's strengths

We empathize each other's weaknesses

The Heartbreaker and the Heartbroken

We fit

## LOVERS

Each of you;
The past and the now
Holds the keys to me
The where, the why, the how

You are all the ingredients of my character
Each of you stands alone like
a musical note,
pure and simple.
I dared to blend and
make music with you.
The good, the bad,
the happy, the sad;
The earth quaking, mind-shaking
Evolution of my soul-making
        like a puzzle, all pieces valuable
Without the presence of each
it is not complete

Without you, there is no me.

Without me, you lack part of you

Each piece brings us peace...

...of heart, of body, of mind

I was blessed

that you were my kind


If only for a brief moment in time

We shared love;

 the physical kind

Those that crossed

and cross the emotional line

Are the arteries of my steady beating heart

Your presence an obvious part.


Each of you;

The past and the now

Holds the keys to me

The where, the why, the how...

## ADDICTED

A raindrop falling into a raging sea

If I am painting my compulsions this is what you would see

A raindrop falling into a raging sea

I am a raindrop

Drifting off course without control

     Into the black hole

Feeding the addiction

      instead of the true need

Seeking escape

      letting the fixation take the lead

The vortex is strong and

      I am struggling to get loose of its hold

Praying for a moment of clarity to get free

I am a raindrop

A raindrop falling into a raging sea

# A FATHERLESS GIRL

A Fatherless girl

Became a Fatherless woman

Trying to fill the emptiness and not knowing

How to fill a hole in my life,

    that stemmed from a hole in my soul

How does anyone fill that kind of void?

I've poured liquor in it;

    I've blown smoke in it;

        I've consumed too much food

Nothing fills it

I was only a child when you took your life

    And it changed MY life forever

Colquhoun

You weren't there to show me

how I should be treated

Fatherless girls keep looking for him

in other men's eyes

Hoping a man's love

will make her whole again

Without fatherly guidance

we become prey

We give ourselves away,

Until there is almost nothing left of self

Being abandoned leaves us feeling

we are of little worth

Accepting and believing

in our insignificance

Now I've reach the middle part of life

I don't miss you any less

than I did the day you left


I've learned that the abyss in me

cannot be satisfied

by a person or a thing


The pain is not meant to be numbed

Only I can give me what you could not

I'll be the Father I always deserved

I am not less without you

I am worthy of love and deserving of life

    because I know their value

You gave me life and love and then took them from
    me

Reclaiming both have allowed me to set

    you free

Goodbye Daddy

# MY LIFE, MY RULES

It is a relatively simple concept that few seem to grasp

This is my life

so I get to play by

my rules

So many seem to think that their opinion trumps mine

This is where I draw the line


There was a time when I tried to follow the

blue print of should do's

Tried to be who they said

Ignored that little voice

in my head

**Never**

Ignore

the little voice

It reminds you that it is your choice
Warns you

When danger looms

Dares you

To take the chance

Reminds you

It is all up to you

Whether a triumph or a tragedy

MINE

You are entitled to

Your opinion

I'm not asking for it

Take care of your own life

This is

**MY LIFE**

And they are

**MY RULES**

# I HAVE MY TICKET

You are a foreign land

The language is different and so are the flavors,

     the sites, the sounds

     My imagination abounds

I have my ticket

Fearful because

     you are the unknown

Still seeking because

     you are intriguing

Wanting to know and to explore this

 mystifying realm

I have my ticket

I have no map, no compass

          to guide me

There is no plan, it's just serendipity


I have my ticket


I come forth with my empty canteen and

knap sack

If you wish to fill me and them

The wealth of my soul is yours for the taking

and there is

no mistaking

Such a voyage will transform

    The You and The Me To The We


Take me on this trip

Show me the beauty of this place that I desire,

    whenever I close my eyes to see your face

I have a one-way ticket

# THE GOOD BROTHER

You say you want a BMW

**B**lack **M**an **W**orking, but he better drive

one too


In truth you want so much more

      what is it you are <u>really</u> looking for?

The house, the car, the ring, the bling and

      he best be making you sing

Before you settle on a thing

Take your shades off and listen to what I say

You may have seen the right man

      but never given him the time of day

You may have walked right by not noticing

 the content and depth of his character

What **you** seek **you** <u>will</u> find,

But rest assured you are <u>blind</u> if you went past

The Good Brother


He was right there - Serves God - Served his country;

He knows what it is to be a man; He does all he can


Sometimes it is hard to face it all,

       but face it he does...

          and that <u>includes</u> his mistakes

          Not afraid to lend a helping hand

          to his fellow man

He won't judge you

       and **<u>knows</u>** how to love you

Take another look at those deep dark eyes

      he has nothing to hide

When your heart is full you will never want for more;

How and why would you settle for *anyone* less?

      and let me stress...


You can keep your BMW – the ring, the bling

I know the difference between what is real

      and what are <u>just</u> things

<u>I</u> celebrate the <u>real</u> Good Brother

Now you can put those shades back on

your face

      now that I've made my case

Keep your eyes and your heart open

      and you will be celebrating

            the Good Brother too


Praise to all the Good Brothers

      each and every one of you

# GLORY

Copper skin and wooly hair

The sun your glory

Charcoal eyes resilient

Reflecting wisdom

Your pigment a badge

Of honor, of pain

Spirit – Infinite

Strength – Unbreakable

They cannot disgrace you

...so they try to erase you

Copper skin and wooly hair

Your genocide I cannot bear

The SON your glory

# LION HEART

You, the one with the Lion heart, you have slayed dragons and walked through fires for me.

You have loved me unconditionally.

You are my home, my heart, my family.

You showed me life is messy and love is complicated, and that prepared me for what life's thrown at me.

You helped me earn my Ph.D in common sense, and you were right it is a valuable degree.

I am watching you age gracefully; and remembering everything you've taught me.

We often walked towards the sunset and all its promise for tomorrow, never losing sight of the present day and making it the best day possible, just in case there wasn't a tomorrow.

You are all that I aspire to be.

Your Lion Heart beats inside of me.

## SOUL CONNECTION

Recognition

Your eyes reflected it

Absorbing the ease with which the gaze

was returned,

     A longing satisfied

As an adopted child yearns for their face

     Mirrored  in another's;

A displaced soul seeks its spiritual family.

An open heart and an open mind

     guide our steps.

We seek understanding and peace.

No unity in labels,

     they divide and conquer us.

Soar like an eagle!

Let our spirits carry us to freedom;

     To resolution,

Where all can see what is reality.

...and then we will really LIVE

# US

Music plays.

Our soundtrack... retro 80's

Comfortable and familiar

Like a favorite pair of jeans

A soft place to fall

Here words or silences

require no explanation

Communicating with a glance

What could not be conveyed to others

in a lifetime

Similarities reflected

Differences complimentary

Siblings without rivalry
Best Friends

# TICK TICK TICK

Tick tick tick

Spring came early

The snow drops and crocuses broke through in February

Barely into March

        and the streets are lined with trees

        full of fluffy pink cherry blossoms

Tick tick tick

The clock is set to "spring" forward

What exactly is the daylight saved for?

Tick tick tick

Youth waste time wanting age

Aged waste time longing for youth

Tick tick tick

What about today?

The seconds, the minutes, the hours?

What was accomplished?

Tick tick tick

The days go by

Tick tick tick

Still living for when the clock dictates release

Still looking at a day timer longing for the weekend

Still looking at a calendar at the days booked "off"

Tick tick tick

Years have passed

Wonder where the time went?

Time cast out like the baby with the bathwater

Like being 44 and knowing your fertility is no more

Mind the time

Before you lose your mind

Tick tick tick

Time

Is

UP.

# ALL I HAVE ARE TEARS

I greeted the world with a smile

Only to have the shit kicked

     out of me

Today is one of those

     shit kicking days

Joy and hope are only words

If you don't have any feelings attached to them,

Only words, no point of reference

I tried today

     I tried to smile

         All I have are tears

Joy and hope feel like a secret

     that no one will share with me

Today, the more I give

     the more the world will take

There is nothing left inside of me

       but these tears

For all the years that I tried,

Tried to believe

Believe that joy existed,

Existed if I was only patient

Try to hope

Without hope we are nothing

       but empty shells

Maybe if I still have tears to give

       I'm not empty

# MEMORY FOAM

I heard a song on the radio


It was playing the last time we touched

Our eyes spoke more than any words

    we'll ever say


Unconsciously I brush my finger tips over where you
grazed my flesh

The skin reacting like memory foam


Chill bumps raise up and all the little hairs stand up
charged with static electricity

Physical responses to a memory


Thoughts of you cut through me

like white noise through background sound

The passion lives, even when you are not around

        Just

           Below

               the surface...

It allows life to go on at its regular pace but

waits like a thief in the night for any chance for some carnal romance


A friend once shared that in exchange for an opportunity to see her lover again,

she would surrender a year of her life

I understand,

For you touch me better than I can


You kiss me like we've been lovers, lifetime after lifetime


I smiled to myself and hoped you were listening to this song too

I say out loud

This one's for YOU

# RECOVERING FROM BRAIN SURGERY

Up and down like a roller coaster

Moods and pills

Hurry up and wait for the healing

It takes time they say

No time for that

Those words are old and worn like my patience

I want a new day

Turn the switch

Let me feel the luminosity

The ideas are waiting to light up inside of me

I am ready to be lifted up

Waiting

Slowly

Healing

Up and down like a roller coaster

Moods and pills

I'm recovering from brain surgery

What's your excuse?

# THE SLOW GOODBYE

We were close, closer than most

Sometimes that meant lines were crossed

And sometimes we didn't know

they were crossed

Until actions couldn't be undone

Words couldn't be unsaid

Then like a plane you started your descent

It was a slow goodbye

You left piece by piece

In your lucid moments

You were able to communicate

You didn't like this place

Like you knew your memory

was being erased

It made me appreciate

that we had been close, closer than most

Maybe somewhere in your DNA you knew

Time was of the essence
You were able to enjoy your grandchildren

You saw me find happiness

And as the clock was ticking down...

I found out that you were glad I had

That knowledge was liberating


Our relationship had its share of trials

but never lacked love

Love and Life, so many unexpected twists
and turns

As I sat with you in your silence,
I was able to find the words
To tell you everything

Then both you and I could let go
And finally end this slow goodbye
As ready as I thought I was for you to find
peace
I am still struggling

We were close, closer than most

I'll carry the good memories
and release the rest
I hope you did the same
I'll find you in the light
I know your love will call my name

## A MESSAGE FROM GREAT-GREAT GRANDMOTHER LOUCINDIA

I was tired and I wanted to go home

 I wanted to fly away

I closed my eyes as if to sleep

      as if to dream and I flew away

Finally flying and seeing the world for real

      instead of just in my imagination

I'm flying high above

I'm not tired anymore

The last couple of years

as my mind lost its sharp edges

      I found myself leaving my house

I was trying to get back home

      all I wanted was to go home

Home to Mississippi to be with my family:

my mother, my father, my brothers,

my sisters, and my child

I wanted to go fishing

I wanted to ride horses bareback as I had as a child

I'm flying over mountains and streams

I'm flying over oceans and forests

I'm flying everywhere to see my family

      the ones here with me

           and the ones I've left on earth

I'm flying high above - I'm not tired anymore


I breath the air not just through my nose and mouth

      I take in the breath beyond my lungs,

I breathe with my spirit

 My spirit flies and I am home

… And I am with you with every breath

I love you all

# YOU WERE WITH ME ALL ALONG

You were with me all along

With your Beautiful Eccentricity

You had a message for me

Why try to be a crow

when a peacock you clearly be

Pass on the porridge

if passion fruit is your other choice

Always listen to your little voice


Seeds of wisdom that were subtle

and quietly grew

Like a secret between me & you

Three decades we traveled in our own separate lives

I thought of you often - I wondered if you knew?

**the flower grew**

A hybrid of belief & strength, rainbow in color...


In Gratitude I released the seeds into the wind

Wild & Free – Like YOU, Like ME

A gift that increases in value

by passing it on

**You were with me all along**


I see souls who need encouragement

for their flower to grow

I'm right there to tend what has been sown

Now fate has brought us together again.

I gaze at your face & I know

you made the world a better place-

For me and for all of us who weren't so strong...


**You were with me all along...**

# LADY ON THE PARK BENCH

The smile that rests

Behind the lady's tired eyes

Speaks to me of springtime

    and love lost

The joy of the earth

    when she was in her youth

Cherry blossoms, gentle breezes,

    the soft life giving rain,

The earth's beauty in life's springtime

Now like a statue

    she sits on the bench in the park

        in the autumn of her life

The gallant Prince never came


Even in her dreams

    His shiny is armour tainted with age

And his horse is old and feeble

Her heart, like winter is frozen.

Her smile, like tears, washed away.

# ROYAL AND BLUE

Royal Blue Velvet Dress
You adorned my curves
    with grace and decadence
Held close and breathed in
I detect the faint scent of sin
Closer still I let it touch my skin
I feel the ghosts of old lovers
Quilted invisibly within
A dated photo wearing the dress
So different this woman
Her values a mess
The dress
Still beautiful, velvet and blue
But she and it don't fit
The seams burst,
    not so much from the girth,
        more from worth
Arriving here because of
    my wit and that is the most comfortable fit
I am Royal, always was and always will be
All that already existed inside of me
The time has come to toss the dress

## PAINTING:

**Sally Suh**
Royal and Blue (cover art)
Lotus Flower (inspired by photo taken by Kari Gunderson)

**Photographs:**

**Luanne Morley**
Horse Eye (Stupid Humans)
Raven (Spirit Thief)
Trees at Dawn (When Dreams Meet Daylight)
Raging Sea (Addicted)

**Melody Fowler**
Lady on a Park Bench

**Sketches:**

**Diana Colquhoun**
Rose (Fatherless Girl)
Flying Spirit (Message from Great Grandmother)
Flower Fairy (You were with me All Along)

## Special thanks to:

My mentor, the incredible Miss Diana Colquhoun:
You recognized the artist inside of me
and brought her into the light!
"You were with me all along."
I cherish your contributions to the book and to my life!


Lou Dubois, your gentle nature helped me heal;

Joan Pescott, you taught me poetry doesn't have to
rhyme.  You also taught me that confidence is powerful
and sexy;

Luanne Morley for your photo contributions, you
captured perfectly what was between the lines.
Truly my sister and my BFF!

Deborah McNicol for sharing your artist's instinct;
"You rock babe!"


Sally Suh for the cover and the lotus flower,
You understood;
Passion has both light and darkness.

·

Susan Suh, you are my guide, my friend and an
incredible visionary.  You will always be my little girl
even if you are an old soul.

Arric for his heart.

**MELODY** lives in the picturesque and tranquil British Columbia, Canada, just outside the city of Vancouver.

Her writing experience has fundamentally been as a wordsmith for letters and articles: polishing corporate reports for others. Then, after being involved in the development of an independent film, her creativity stirred. She stepped outside the confines of business writing and her artistic spirit was born, and with it her joy.

She writes fiction, but her true passion is poetry because it speaks the heart's universal language. She is inspired by the works of Maya Angelou, Alice Walker, Charles Bukowski and fellow Canadian Shane Koyczan because they embrace all aspects of human behavior and of life. Melody believes life itself is her greatest muse.

Her insightful reflections leave you with the sensation that she has reached into your heart, held your feelings in her hands, and then lets her pen tell your story, and often hers.

Manufactured by Amazon.ca
Acheson, AB

13117381R00069